HUMAN RITES

Seth Rozin

BROADWAY PLAY PUBLISHING INC
New York
www.broadwayplaypub.com
info@broadwayplaypub.com

Cover photo by Plate 3

First edition: March 2019
I S B N: 978-0-88145-829-9

Book design: Marie Donovan
Page make-up: Adobe InDesign
Typeface: Palatino

HUMAN RITES received its world premiere at Phoenix Theatre in Indianapolis from 20 July–13 August 2017. The cast and creative contributors were:

ALAN FRIEDMAN ....Rob Johansen
MICHAELA RICHARDS ....Milicent Wright
LYDIA NAMANDU .... Paeton Chavis

Director ....Lavina Jadhwani
Set design .... Bernie Killian
Costume design .... Deb Sargent
Lighting design .... Zac Hunter
Sound design ....Ben Dobler

HUMAN RITES received its East Coast premiere at InterAct Theatre Company in Philadelphia from 23 March–15 April 2018. The cast and creative contributors were:

ALAN FRIEDMAN ....Joe Guzman
MICHAELA RICHARDS .... Kimberly S Fairbanks
LYDIA NAMANDU ....Lynnette R Freeman

Director .... Harriet Power
Set design .... Colin McIlvaine
Costume design ....Lizzy Pecora
Lighting design ....Jerold Forsythe
Sound design .... Daniel Kontz

The playwright wishes to thank
Fuambai Sia Ahmadu and **Richard Shweder**,
whose life and work served as inspiration for the play.

The playwright also wishes to thank the following for
their invaluable contributions to the development of
this play:

Sasha Bratt & Playhouse on Park
Caroline Clay
Brian Earp
Tom Gibbons
Janet Goldwater
Susan Gurman
Maura Krause
Bridget O'Leary
Kittson O'Neill
Harriet Power
Sabrina Profitt
Virginia Valian

CHARACTERS & SETTING

ALAN FRIEDMAN, *early 50s, Caucasian, tenured cultural psychologist at a major university. A true intellectual who lacks some social graces and can easily default to smug or petulant.*

MICHAELA RICHARDS, *late 40s, African American, Dean of Arts & Sciences at the same university. An impressive thinker and leader whose well-cultivated formality doesn't eclipse her warmth, passion or sense of humor.*

LYDIA NAMANDU, *mid–late 20s, a member of the Kono people of Sierra Leone, currently a doctoral candidate in anthropology at the same university. A powerful mind that has yet to find its voice. She speaks with an accent, but in most ways appears like a Western graduate student.*

Time: The present

Place: The office of the Dean of Arts & Sciences at a major American university.

For my father,
Paul Rozin,
who instilled in me the value of critical thinking.

(The office of the Dean of Arts & Sciences at a major American university. The room is as elegant as it is impressive: a rich, wood floor is partially obscured by a couple of sumptuous rugs from the Middle-East; bookshelves are neatly filled with academic books, awards, framed photographs and ethnographic artifacts from around the world; fabric wall-hangings on the walls and one Sri Lankan cobra mask. In one part of the room, next to an arched window overlooking campus green, is a handsome writing table with a laptop computer, along with a telephone and various neat stacks of papers and files. Behind the desk is a leather swivel chair. In front of the desk are a couple of chairs for guests.)

(Late afternoon sunlight streams into the room, creating moving shadows of trees gently swaying in the breeze.)

(ALAN FRIEDMAN, wearing the academic's uniform—a tweedy sport coat, button-down shirt and jeans—stands, looking around, a little nervous. His gaze lands on the mask. After a moment, MICHAELA RICHARDS enters with authority, moving briskly by him. She is on her cell phone, wearing an outfit that conveys professionalism, accented by a hint of African jewelry.)

MICHAELA: *(Into the phone)* I have a meeting now. I know. I'll be home by six, six-fifteen at the latest. Okay. Love you, bye. *(To ALAN)* Hello, Alan. Sorry I'm late.

ALAN: Hi. No problem.

MICHAELA: This business with the Inuit students wanting to be recognized by the Asian American Studies Program is requiring a lot of my time.

ALAN: I didn't know there were enough Inuit students on campus to form a caucus.

MICHAELA: There are two students and one assistant professor.

ALAN: *(Laughs to himself)* Okay...

MICHAELA: Exactly.

ALAN: Well, I say "good for them!"

MICHAELA: So do I. I just wish I could spend more of my time on academic matters and less of my time as a referee.

(ALAN laughs.)

MICHAELA: Some of these fights over fiefdoms are awfully petty.

ALAN: That's why I never wanted to be Chair of my department. I'm happy to leave squabbles over our fiefdom to the more ambitious fiefs!

MICHAELA: There's a lot of wisdom in that decision.

(Beat)

ALAN: You look great.

MICHAELA: Thank you.

(Slightly awkward beat)

ALAN: And a lovely office.

MICHAELA: It's from Sri Lanka.

ALAN: What?

MICHAELA: The mask you were looking at. Naga Raksha, the cobra mask. It was a gift from one of my colleagues there, who helped me navigate the utter chaos that is Sri Lankan bureaucracy.

ALAN: That's right. You studied the Kaffirs?

MICHAELA: I did. For two and a half years.

ALAN: Fascinating people.

MICHAELA: Do you think so?

ALAN: Well, I mean, just the history alone. All we ever hear about is the slave trade to the new world, but a handful of Africans were taken by the Portuguese to Sri Lanka…

MICHAELA: More than a handful.

ALAN: I just meant, in relative terms, the numbers were small.

(MICHAELA *holds her gaze on* ALAN.)

ALAN: Unless there's something you know that I don't, which, given that you *lived* with them, wouldn't surprise me.

MICHAELA: The numbers were *relatively small*.

ALAN: And you were doing genomic research, is that right?

MICHAELA: The Kaffirs lived in reproductive isolation for several generations. I was interested in the degree of variation within their genetic population, and comparing it with tribes that remain in the part of Africa where they were taken from.

ALAN: Important work.

MICHAELA: Is it?

ALAN: I think so.

MICHAELA: Well. That makes about five of us.

(ALAN *offers a knowing smile.*)

MICHAELA: How's the family?

ALAN: The family's, uh, good. The kids are, well, mostly, they're out of the house now. Robyn, my oldest, just started grad school for social work, and

Eric's at Northwestern. So Kathy and I, we— We're adjusting to that…

MICHAELA: Your wife is well?

ALAN: Uh, yeah. Well… Kathy's— She's been on different meds, and things have been, you know, in and out since…

MICHAELA: I understand.

(Beat)

ALAN: And you?

MICHAELA: I'm not on any meds.

ALAN: I wasn't suggesting—

MICHAELA: A joke, Alan.

ALAN: Right.

MICHAELA: I've been well. I have a daughter.

ALAN: Really?! Wow, that's…

MICHAELA: I adopted her. From Mali. When she was twenty-two months old. Shortly after we—

ALAN: Ah, okay…

MICHAELA: I was thirty-six, recently tenured. My workload was intense. I wanted a child, but I was too busy to continue banging my head against a wall with all manner of men. So, I decided to embrace my independence, and save at least one girl from some of the horrors that awaited her.

ALAN: That's…terrific! I didn't know you wanted—

MICHAELA: Yes.

ALAN: You've always seemed so…

MICHAELA: What? *Un*-motherly?

ALAN: No. God no! Just— So busy with your career…

MICHAELA: I always wanted children.

ALAN: Well… Congratulations!

MICHAELA: Thank you. Her name is Naila. She's a sophomore in high school. Says she wants to be a poet.

ALAN: Good for her.

MICHAELA: I don't think being a poet is good for anyone, but thanks for the vote of support. *(With sarcastic disdain.)* Last week she came home with her *nose pierced!* That is one thing I will never understand.

ALAN: For me, it was the tattoo.

MICHAELA: *(Nods, in agreement)* That's another one.

ALAN: *(Shrugs.)* They have to make their own choices.

MICHAELA: Yes, they do. That's sewn into the fabric of our culture, isn't it? One of our unassailable values. Children being empowered to choose their own path.

ALAN: I suppose so.

MICHAELA: *(Looks at* ALAN, *but keeps her thought to herself.)* Hmm.

ALAN: This is, uhm…

MICHAELA: *(Refers to the mask)* You're a collector, aren't you? Mostly African, if memory serves.

ALAN: Amateur collector, but yes. I've got about thirty at home.

MICHAELA: I remember a few of them in your office, along with a large, free-standing fertility figure.

ALAN: Yup…

MICHAELA: I found that surprising and attractive at the time.

*(*ALAN *smiles, not sure if that was meant as a compliment.* MICHAELA *looks at* ALAN, *squarely, for the first time, smiles. Somewhat formal, yet genuine)*

MICHAELA: It's good to see you, Alan.

ALAN: Likewise.

MICHAELA: It's been what? Twelve, thirteen years?

ALAN: We've been at a few meetings, faculty receptions—

MICHAELA: Of course.

ALAN: And I came to your lecture—the one on women in the Antilles—

MICHAELA: Antigua.

ALAN: Right, sorry. Just after you took over as Dean. I came over to say hi at the reception.

MICHAELA: I remember.

ALAN: And I wrote you a note when I heard about your appointment.

MICHAELA: Yes. I just meant… Being in a room together. Alone.

ALAN: Ah…

(Beat)

MICHAELA: A lot of water under the bridge.

ALAN: Yes. For you, especially.

MICHAELA: For me? Why?

ALAN: Just—I mean, I've been doing the same thing forever, and my personal life, you know… But you-- Not that there's anything surprising about your career trajectory.

MICHAELA: You thought I would be a Dean? God knows I never thought about it.

ALAN: You seemed—when you arrived here, at least— fairly ambitious.

MICHAELA: You think so?

ALAN: Yes…

MICHAELA: Well. I had to be. Back in college I was one of a handful of Black students—

ALAN: I remember you telling me...

MICHAELA: —and an even smaller minority of *one* Black biology major.

ALAN: And now you're a Dean!

MICHAELA: Yes...

ALAN: Anyway, it suits you well. A position of real academic leadership. *(Jokingly formal)* I'm honored to have you as my superior.

MICHAELA: *(With an inscrutable smile)* You always did like me on top.

ALAN: *(Slightly flustered)* Uhhh...

MICHAELA: And how are your parents? I don't think I met them while we were—?

ALAN: No! Definitely not. They're, uh...well, they're getting old is what they are. My father's losing his hearing and my mother's kind of worn out managing him, so about a year ago my sisters and I pitched in and set them up in an assisted living facility.

MICHAELA: That's good of you...

ALAN: Yeah, they've got really good food there. It's a very social place. They even have a little theatre...

MICHAELA: My mother, Milicent—Millie—

ALAN: *(He does not remember.)* Okay...

MICHAELA: Whenever I say to her "Look, mom, I think it's time to" —she cuts me off with "Don't you even *think* about putting me in a home!"

(ALAN laughs, knowingly.)

MICHAELA: She's been doing it alone for so long, she thinks she can handle anything.

(Beat)

ALAN: So… You asked to see me.

MICHAELA: I did, yes.

(Beat)

ALAN: I just-- I think there's someone waiting outside, so I—

MICHAELA: I'm aware, thanks.

(Beat)

ALAN: Are you going to tell me *why* you wanted to see me?

MICHAELA: I assumed it was obvious.

ALAN: In my twenty-one years at this esteemed university, no Dean has ever *summoned* me.

MICHAELA: Well. How does it feel?

ALAN: I'm not sure I—

MICHAELA: You were probably never called into the Principal's office in high school, were you?

ALAN: Uh, no…

MICHAELA: No detentions for Alan Friedman.

ALAN: Can you just tell me why I'm here?

MICHAELA: You really don't know?

ALAN: No…

MICHAELA: Wow. Okay.

ALAN: Like I said, this is the first time—

MICHAELA: Yes, I got that. So what *did* you expect?

ALAN: I…thought, maybe, you wanted some inside scoop on my department, or, maybe, I don't know, you wanted to…*re*… *(He looks at* MICHAELA *suggestively.)* I really had no idea…

MICHAELA: No. You didn't.

(Beat)

ALAN: I think the last time was October, [2005] *(Thirteen years prior to current year).*

MICHAELA: What?

ALAN: The last time we were in a room together. Alone. Late October, [2005].

MICHAELA: *(With a slight laugh)* Okay…

ALAN: What?

MICHAELA: I'm just—

ALAN: You're surprised I remember?

MICHAELA: A little.

ALAN: Memory's a funny thing.

MICHAELA: Yes, it is…I imagine we have very different memories of that…time.

ALAN: Mine are…very positive.

MICHAELA: I'm sure they are.

ALAN: Very fond memories.

MICHAELA: I'm glad.

ALAN: I mean, apart from the fact that I was, you know…

MICHAELA: Committing adultery?

ALAN: *(Reflexively defensive)* Hey! Jesus!

(MICHAELA holds her gaze. ALAN squirms.)

ALAN: Uhm, look…

MICHAELA: Hmmm?

ALAN: It's—

MICHAELA: What—?

ALAN: I'm just— Maybe we should find another time to—

MICHAELA: *(Picks up the letter from her desk and hands it to* ALAN.*)* Here.

ALAN: What's this?

MICHAELA: I gather you presented a paper of yours in class last week.

ALAN: I-- Yes. That's a pretty standard practice…

MICHAELA: The paper asserted some controversial findings.

ALAN: Yes.

MICHAELA: And it upset your students.

ALAN: How would you know that? Did they—? Did they come to you?

MICHAELA: *(Refers to the letter)* Your students co-signed a letter to me. They want you to retract your claims.

ALAN: That's…ridiculous. Why are you even…?

MICHAELA: I support their sentiments.

ALAN: What?!

MICHAELA: I met with them on Tuesday, listened to their concerns, and while I, of course, respect and *champion* academic freedom, I agree with them.

ALAN: You agr—?!

MICHAELA: I think you might want to consider retracting the paper.

ALAN: I've submitted it for publication.

MICHAELA: You could *un*submit it.

ALAN: This is not just another paper, Michaela. This is going to be the *central* chapter in my book. The culmination of my work as a cultural psychologist.

MICHAELA: That's unfortunate.

ALAN: You heard about my research, *second hand*, from a bunch of *undergraduates*, and based on that—

MICHAELA: I read the paper.

ALAN: You read the paper?! How did you—? My students sent it to you?!

MICHAELA: They were upset. They *are* upset.

ALAN: *(Manages his anger)* And you're asking me, as the Dean of Arts & Sciences, to retract my work?!

MICHAELA: I'm simply suggesting you consider that, yes.

ALAN: *(Almost speechless at the absurdity of it)* Wh—?! *(Opens his arms, looks directly at* MICHAELA. *With sarcastic formality.)* No. I will not retract my work. I stand by my findings.

MICHAELA: Well, then…

ALAN: *(Incredulous)* Do you—?

MICHAELA: What?

ALAN: This is hardly within the purview of your job.

MICHAELA: I'm just responding to a complaint from students.

ALAN: You could've emailed me, or— You *called me in here* to ask me to retract my work?! If I took this to the Provost—

MICHAELA: We're just having a conversation, Alan.

ALAN: And given our history. I mean, you *know* me.

MICHAELA: Our history that you don't want the Provost to know about?

(ALAN realizes he's caught.)

MICHAELA: The students could have gone to the paper.

ALAN: Okay…?

MICHAELA: They could have gone about this in a much more public and impulsive way. Considering how upset they are.

ALAN: So, what? I should applaud their relative maturity? Fine! Good for them! I'm proud to be teaching students who are so put off by evidence that does not comport with their *nineteen years* of life experience that they *tattle* on me to the Dean instead of to the press!

MICHAELA: I don't think you understand the—

ALAN: This is a sophomore seminar. I used my own research to illustrate the challenges of investigating other cultural perspectives. I knew the students would find it difficult to accept my conclusions. That was the point! But the *evidence supports the conclusions.*

MICHAELA: Your "data," your extensive field research in Sub-Saharan Africa—

ALAN: Sierra Leone, The Gambia, Mali—

MICHAELA: —shows, *conclusively*, that female genital mutilation—

ALAN: *(Corrects her.)* Circumcision.

MICHAELA: —*mutilation* is embraced and endorsed by most of the women who practice it.

ALAN: Absolutely. With some variation, from one group to another, obviously.

(Beat)

MICHAELA: As I said. I agree with the students. *(Refers to the letter)* I believe they referred to your paper as "misguided and toxic."

(ALAN laughs derisively.)

MICHAELA: Something funny about that?

ALAN: Misguided and toxic?

MICHAELA: I think those words are extremely well-chosen.

ALAN: Michaela: My paper is not one of these ill-informed fringe rants in the blogosphere by some nobody looking for his fifteen minutes of fame. This is *your field*. This is science.

MICHAELA: Science can't be misguided or toxic?

ALAN: I suppose it can be, if it's found to be *bad* science.

MICHAELA: *(Eyebrows raised)* Well.

(Beat)

ALAN: I'm stunned. I really can't believe that you—! *(He moves away, angrily.)*

MICHAELA: What? You can't believe I expected you to capitulate? I didn't. I don't. Unless you've really softened in your middle age.

ALAN: *(He shakes his head and laughs to himself.)* Maybe my students don't understand what it means to be a tenured professor—

MICHAELA: They're not that naïve—

ALAN: But *you*, Michaela… I mean, they know there's nothing you can force me to do, right?

(MICHAELA looks intently at ALAN.)

MICHAELA: What do your wife and daughter think of your research?

ALAN: Can we please not—?

MICHAELA: They're women. I'm guessing they're liberal—

ALAN: What Kathy and Robyn think doesn't—

MICHAELA: I know so little about your family.

ALAN: *(To himself)* Thank god…

MICHAELA: Not even pictures on your desk.

ALAN: I was…trying to keep the two of you—

MICHAELA: You were being thoughtful. You didn't want me to see your wife's smiling face while we were fucking on your office couch.

ALAN: *(Barely audible)* I didn't want her smiling face to see *you.*

MICHAELA: *(Shakes her head in disgust)* Nice.

ALAN: I still can't believe I cheated on Kathy for eleven months.

MICHAELA: Why? It's practically an American pastime.

ALAN: I…

MICHAELA: She's not Black, is she?

ALAN: Uh…

MICHAELA: You never told me, but I assumed.

ALAN: That's an odd question.

MICHAELA: Is it?

ALAN: She's a mix of English and Dutch…

MICHAELA: Hmm.

ALAN: Why are you—?

MICHAELA: Just curious.

ALAN: Okay…

MICHAELA: You seemed to have such a *thing* for me back then.

ALAN: Is there a point you're—

MICHAELA: Just curious, Alan. Something I've wondered about.

(Beat)

ALAN: You know what? I clearly, uh, misunderstood—
*(He hands her the letter, puts his anger away and feigns
formality.)* Thank you for the invitation to…whatever!
But I respectfully decline. *(He turns to leave.)*

MICHAELA: What did you misunderstand?

ALAN: *(Turns back)* I— Nothing. I just—I thought
maybe you wanted to…

MICHAELA: To…?

ALAN: Reconnect.

MICHAELA: You mean *rekindle*?

ALAN: Well… Yes.

MICHAELA: I'm surprised. I would have thought you'd
moved on.

ALAN: I have, or, well…I *had*, but… We saw each other
two or three times a week for almost a year.

MICHAELA: Mmhmm.

ALAN: And *you* were the one who ended things.

MICHAELA: Because you couldn't make a decision
about whether to stay in your marriage.

ALAN: Kathy was battling her depression. *Still is.* The
kids were at a tricky age, and—

MICHAELA: *(Puts her hand up to interrupt him)* I
remember all that, Alan. And I got to a point where
I'd had enough of that nonsense and wanted to have
a family of my own. *(Beat)* I think I made the right
decision. You're still with your wife and I have a
daughter.

ALAN: *(Deflated, nods)* Yeah… *(He sits in a chair.)*

MICHAELA: That letter from your students got me
thinking.

ALAN: About what?

MICHAELA: The masks in your office—all those eyes, those faces, *African* faces—on every wall. Each one representing some myth; some god; some ancient human rite or ritual. All those African eyes watching us, as we coupled like wild animals in heat. Imagine if those masks could talk.

ALAN: I'd really rather not.

MICHAELA: I'm sorry. I'm poking at old wounds.

ALAN: I still don't see…

MICHAELA: What?

ALAN: You called me into your office because of my *students*? I mean, I'm not surprised they're up in arms, but I would think you get letters like these—

MICHAELA: *Your paper offends me, Alan.* As a scientist. As a woman. As a thinking, feeling human being. Your paper offends me.

ALAN: So, you're—

MICHAELA: So, I'm asking you, as a friend to a friend—

ALAN: As a friend?!

MICHAELA: As one colleague to another, I'm *advising* you to consider the repercussions of—

ALAN: Wow! I—

MICHAELA: You'll be a pariah, Alan. Here on campus and in your field. You'll be that crackpot professor we hear about at *other* universities.

ALAN: So, you're just looking out for my professional reputation.

MICHAELA: Now, you're being petulant.

ALAN: Let me worry about my reputation, thank you.

MICHAELA: It's not just *your* reputation, Alan.

ALAN: Ah! You don't want to be known as the Dean who *enables* the crackpot professor!

MICHAELA: I have not enabled you.

ALAN: I don't think you actually *read* my paper.

MICHAELA: Of course I did.

ALAN: So, what? You just dismissed it? I would think, as a fellow scientist, you might be surprised by the data.

MICHAELA: I wasn't.

ALAN: *(Confused)* You weren't surprised…

MICHAELA: Well. Knowing the author as I do.

ALAN: You're treating me like I'm some kind of right wing religious fanatic who's hawking Creationism to impressionable students on College Green! My paper is based on actual, reputable, methodical research.

MICHAELA: I don't believe that.

ALAN: Because you don't like what I found?

MICHAELA: Because I don't like what you *think* you found.

ALAN: What I *think* I—?! *(He moves away, shocked. Pause)* I was not seeking these results, Michaela.

MICHAELA: *(Skeptical)* Okay…

ALAN: Is that what you think?

MICHAELA: Why did you set out to study them?

ALAN: What do you—?! I'm a cultural psychologist.

MICHAELA: Yes, but why *them*?

ALAN: I was interested in the psychology of these women who—

MICHAELA: Why African women?

ALAN: I told you. I—

MICHAELA: There are people all over the world who submit to all kinds of primitive and demeaning practices. Why not study underage sex workers in Southeast Asia? Women of *any* age in Saudi Arabia? Mormon women who submit themselves to polygamous husbands? Sub-Saharan *men* who submit themselves to scarification?

ALAN: I don't know what you're suggesting. Why did you study the Kaffirs?

MICHAELA: I'm a black woman. I was interested in other black women.

ALAN: Well, that's great. I didn't feel compelled to study people who share my pigmentation.

MICHAELA: Of course not.

ALAN: Meaning what?

MICHAELA: Meaning you feel perfectly comfortable studying everybody else. That's pretty much the definition of privilege.

ALAN: I'm willing to bet that no one – not your thesis advisor, not your department chair, *no one* – told you your research had to be confined to the African diaspora.

MICHAELA: I'm not talking about rules, Alan. I'm talking about what *feels* allowed. A concept you can't even imagine.

ALAN: So you're what? Jealous? Resentful that I don't feel *limited* to—

MICHAELA: Please!

ALAN: Jesus, Michaela! I didn't want this fight.

MICHAELA: No?

ALAN: No! Like *you*, like most *thinking, feeling* people I assumed that the practice of female circumcision—

MICHAELA: Mutilation.

ALAN: —*circumcision* was barbaric, humiliating, dangerous and disempowering.

MICHAELA: Bully for you.

ALAN: I wanted to investigate the *psychology* of these people, these *women*—

MICHAELA: Girls!

ALAN: Yes, girls!

MICHAELA: Younger than my own!

ALAN: Yes. Who submitted to such a— Such a heinous practice.

MICHAELA: And yet you found that a few of them articulated plausible, if primitive reasons for doing so.

ALAN: What I learned, Michaela, by interviewing over four hundred women—members of six different ethnic groups in four different countries—girls who were preparing for the ritual, as well as older women who had already been initiated and were now preparing their daughters for the same ritual, even the women who conducted the actual surgeries—what I learned is that a decisive majority of them not only embrace the practice, enthusiastically, but consider it a fundamentally good thing; socially, spiritually, physically and aesthetically.

MICHAELA: And I find that hard to believe.

ALAN: Hard to believe or hard to accept?

(MICHAELA *shows no signs of softening.*)

ALAN: Look. I know this flies in the face of the narrative that's been embraced by everyone in Europe and the U S; the "anti-F G M" movement is incredibly aggressive and successful. And I believed it all! But as it turns out, my research shows that that narrative is incomplete, at best.

MICHAELA: There's been legislation enacted by all kinds of international organizations. The U N, UNICEF's Tostan program. Nigeria and Somalia just banned the practice. And it's a felony here in the U S!

ALAN: But very few serious scholars have bothered to actually *study* the rite of female circumcision.

MICHAELA: Until you rode in on your majestic white horse.

ALAN: What?!

MICHAELA: I can think of several studies published in—

ALAN: Yeah, in progressive journals and activist websites, am I right? Trust me, they're not *scientific* studies. I reviewed them, Michaela. They barely qualify as studies.

MICHAELA: Why should I trust that you—?

ALAN: Because I made the same assumption that *you* did, and—

MICHAELA: You say that, but—

ALAN: No one has done the work my students and I did of interviewing hundreds of women who engage in the practice. Even the phrase "female genital mutilation" was coined, from afar, by Westerners with little knowledge of the actual initiation rite. And it's taken on a life of its own. We just accepted all that as fact, and jumped on the "anti-F G M" bandwagon.

MICHAELA: You sound like a true convert.

ALAN: I'm not *advocating* the practice.

MICHAELA: How civilized of you!

ALAN: I wouldn't want my daughter to be circumcised, but—

MICHAELA: I would hope not!

ALAN: But we have to respect cultural differences.

MICHAELA: So, if a group of people practices slave ownership as an integral part of their culture, we should just accept it?

ALAN: *(Careful)* If the people who are enslaved actively choose to embrace the practice—

MICHAELA: That's a load of shit!

ALAN: Do you know about bug chasing? Gay men pursuing sexual activity with other men who are H I V positive, so that they can contract H I V? They're *choosing* to do it, Michaela, *here in this country!*

MICHAELA: I'm aware, and I find it incomprehensible.

ALAN: Me, too! That's the point! I'm not *advocating* for female circumcision!

MICHAELA: So why not do a study on the bug chasers instead?

ALAN: Would you just, please, read my fucking paper again, *slowly,* so we can discuss the substance of it like two reasonable adult scientists!

(MICHAELA is unwavering. ALAN moves around the room, exercising his frustration.)

ALAN: Do you believe in climate change?

MICHAELA: Of course.

ALAN: You say that as if it's an undisputed fact.

MICHAELA: As far as I'm concerned, it is.

ALAN: Based on what?

MICHAELA: I know where you're headed, Alan, and—

ALAN: Based on *what?*

MICHAELA: Based on decades of evidence, collected by scientists around the world.

ALAN: What about all those deniers who dismiss all that science as bunk? Who say the evidence is a matter of interpretation?

MICHAELA: I believe they're ignorant.

ALAN: They can't abide the facts, because the facts don't support the narrative they're invested in. And you're no different from them, Michaela, if you're just as willing to ignore the evidence.

MICHAELA: I'm not ignoring the evidence. I'm ignoring your paper.

ALAN: Jesus, Michaela! For someone who prides herself on being an independent thinker, you are acting surprisingly like my students, like all the other *sheep*. Not with a thoughtful and considered response, certainly *not* with scientific skepticism.

MICHAELA: I'm skeptical of *your* science.

ALAN: Have you considered the possibility that there is an astonishing cultural divide around the world in attitudes toward female genital surgeries? We feel very personally about this issue.

MICHAELA: *We*?!

ALAN: *Westerners, especially Americans* are repulsed and outraged by the thought of any kind of surgical enhancement to women's genitals.

MICHAELA: It's not enhancement!

ALAN: And our feelings are easily aroused by exaggerated, possibly *invented* stories of torture in other parts of the world. But when you get past all the moralizing and hyperbole, you find that the perception does not always match the reality.

MICHAELA: Says a white man from America.

ALAN: Oh, please!

MICHAELA: What?

ALAN: *(Smiles)* One of the few scientific studies that *does* exist was conducted by a medical anthropologist from Harvard, a *woman*.

MICHAELA: A white woman.

ALAN: Jesus, yes! A white woman! Her research concludes that among women who have been circumcised, medical complications are rare, *and* that most genital alterations are *not* incompatible with sexual enjoyment.

MICHAELA: She wouldn't be the first scientist whose methodology was flawed. Or the last.

ALAN: What?!

MICHAELA: Sometimes our methodology isn't as rigorous as we might want to think it is.

ALAN: You don't know a thing about her methodology. Or mine.

MICHAELA: I know that it doesn't make sense; what *your* rigorous methodology added up to.

(ALAN is speechless.)

MICHAELA: It's not an accident, Alan, that you and I pursued the fields that we did. Your work is important, of course. But the science is a bit fuzzy, isn't it? *I* study concrete, tangible things that can be measured with exquisite precision: The density of bones, the continuity of a genetic code. Whereas you *observe* people, in all their flawed, individual messiness; ask them how they *think* and *feel;* identify trends and patterns in human behavior. And I'm sure your conclusions are *close* to a truth. But your work is never irrefutable, is it? It's always approximations; never precise or absolute; nothing truly measurable. It would be hard to say that the conclusions you and I come to are the same kinds of facts.

ALAN: Wow…I didn't realize you had such disdain for the social sciences.

MICHAELA: Come on, Alan! You have no way of ˙ measuring the degree to which a woman experiences sexual pleasure, circumcised or not. To prove there's no loss in pleasure, you would have had to find a whole lot of women who had had sex before *and after* the procedure. And you'd have to have created some kind of meaningful scale for them to *rate* their pleasure.

ALAN: True enough. But that also means you and all the anti-F G M activists have no way of knowing that there *is* a definitive loss in pleasure. The knife cuts both ways. Pun intended.

MICHAELA: If you remove any part of the clitoris, a woman is going to experience less pleasure.

ALAN: That might be true—

MICHAELA: There's no "might"—

ALAN: —but could also be an exaggerated claim.

MICHAELA: Any diminishment of pleasure is unacceptable!

(ALAN *rolls his eyes in frustration.*)

MICHAELA: Isn't it possible that your accounts from the dozens of African women—

ALAN: Hundreds!

MICHAELA: —were unreliable. Self-reporting is a sketchy enterprise.

ALAN: You have that little respect for our--!

MICHAELA: Or perhaps you never gained the trust of all those women you interviewed, being that you're an *older, white man from America.*

ALAN: *(Overlaps.)* Yes! A white guy from America! I can't tell if you're insinuating that I'm incompetent or racist or both.

MICHAELA: I'm not suggesting either, Alan. But surely, you've experienced the problem of trying to get people of a different culture, a different race, a different gender to give you honest and reliable reports.

ALAN: So, the Kaffirs in Sri Lanka: They naturally trusted *you*.

MICHAELA: More than they would have trusted *you*, I would think.

(Beat)

ALAN: The interviews for my research were conducted by two of my graduate students – Andrea Givens and Sofia Hadhani. And if you think *I* was surprised by what we found, you should have seen their reactions. They were absolutely devastated.

MICHAELA: Good for them.

ALAN: But their findings were the same: In the communities we studied, most African girls and women, mothers and their daughters alike, view circumcision as a spiritual and physical improvement.

MICHAELA: Well. Those African girls and women are—

ALAN: They're what? *(He holds a hard look at her.)* You think two hundred million women are *wrong*. That's an awfully imperialistic—

MICHAELA: Get out of my office.

ALAN: A black American woman with a six-figure salary knows best, huh?

MICHAELA: Get. Out. Of. My. Office.

ALAN: I'm just saying—

MICHAELA: Is there some part of "get out of my office" that baffles you?

ALAN: Wow!

(ALAN *looks at* MICHAELA *with incredulity. She returns his look with a steely glare that might be covering something.*)

(ALAN*'s eyes narrow, a new tack.*)

ALAN: So… What about male circumcision?

MICHAELA: Alan…

ALAN: Male circumcision.

MICHAELA: What about it?

ALAN: Do you think it's equally barbaric to cut off an infant boy's foreskin?

MICHAELA: I don't much care for that practice either.

ALAN: But if you had a son instead of a daughter, you'd want him circumcised, wouldn't you?

MICHAELA: Probably.

ALAN: A little *male* genital mutilation. MGM. Even though the original health reasons for the practice are no longer a legitimate concern? Even though many cultures and religions practice circumcision as a way to curb a *man*'s sexual appetite?

MICHAELA: Alan—

ALAN: The Egyptians. The Jews. *They believed back then* that cutting off the prepuce led to a loss in sexual pleasure *for men.* And we still do it to almost all of our American baby boys, while European boys are enjoying *a lot more pleasure.*

MICHAELA: I'll bet *that*'s an exaggerated claim.

ALAN: And babies don't possess the *capacity* to object to the surgery, as compared with, say, a twelve- year-old girl?

MICHAELA: It's far more *traumatic* for the twelve-year-old girl! And what kind of agency does she really have?

ALAN: Did you know that the hood over the clitoris has the same essential function as the male foreskin?

MICHAELA: Is that a fact?

ALAN: When I began this research, Michaela, I bought this comprehensive human anatomy app to understand everything about the relevant body parts, *in both sexes.* And guess what? The ear lobe, the pinky toe, the appendix are all officially part of the human body, but not the foreskin! So I called the manufacturer, to see if there was an oversight, and they told me the app I bought was designed exclusively for the U S and Israel. The rest of the world uses a version that *includes* the foreskin! So Michaela: where are all the anti-M G M activists?!

MICHAELA: Are you finished?

ALAN: *(He moves to her.)* I don't recall you complaining about *my* being circumcised; you were anything but outraged. Why? Because it's so normal and routine? Because it's widely accepted in our culture? Because it happens to *men*? *(He moves inappropriately close to her, refers to his crotch.)* Or is it because you just liked the look of my—?

MICHAELA: *(As she manages the provocation and the arousal.)* Let's keep your…personal effects…out of this.

ALAN: I think my personal effects are relevant to the case.

MICHAELA: Well, they're not!

(ALAN scrutinizes MICHAELA, then shakes his head and laughs to himself.)

MICHAELA: You find this amusing?

ALAN: I was just…reminded of one of our epic arguments. About gender politics, and I said something, probably flippant, about my genitals being proof of something, and you said, like you just did: "Well, they're not!"

MICHAELA: I remember.

ALAN: We sure had our share of arguments.

MICHAELA: Pre-*and* post-coital.

ALAN: We were not a quiet couple.

MICHAELA: We were not a couple.

ALAN: Right… We were hot for each other.

MICHAELA: We were out of control, is what we were.

ALAN: Yeah…I miss that feeling.

MICHAELA: Do you?

(ALAN *looks at* MICHAELA. *There is something in the air between them. He leans in to kiss her. She pushes him away.*)

MICHAELA: What the hell are you doing?!

ALAN: I'm sorry. I—

(MICHAELA *gathers herself, then sternly:*)

MICHAELA: There it is: Privilege at work!

ALAN: I'm sorry, okay? That was really stupid of me.

MICHAELA: Stupid?

ALAN: Yes! And—

MICHAELA: I think it was more than stupid.

ALAN: But it's got nothing to do with privilege.

MICHAELA: That's *harassment*.

ALAN: Oh, come on!

MICHAELA: You tried to *kiss* me!

ALAN: I know that, but my god--!

MICHAELA: That's a pretty easy line *not* to *cross*.

ALAN: You looked like you were...wanting—

MICHAELA: Don't even try!

ALAN: You did—!

MICHAELA: *(Holds up her hand, admonishingly.)* Alan—!

ALAN: Okay! Okay! Call Campus Security!

MICHAELA: You know: When I received that letter from your students, I thought to myself "of course, Alan must be involved in this!"

ALAN: What do you mean by that?

MICHAELA: Let's just say I was not altogether surprised that it was you at the center of a controversy involving black women.

ALAN: Again, with the suggestion of racism.

MICHAELA: I don't think you're a racist.

ALAN: Thank you!

MICHAELA: But I do believe you have a tendency to exoticize us. *Fetishize* us.

ALAN: What?!

MICHAELA: I think that's what drew you to me, when I first arrived. You came to that colloquium and made a bee-line for me.

ALAN: I— Maybe...

MICHAELA: Oh, you did.

ALAN: You think that I—I exoticize and fetishize black women? That's...

MICHAELA: What?

ALAN: It's ridiculous.

MICHAELA: Is it?

ALAN: Of course it is!

MICHAELA: Then why did you choose to study African women—?

ALAN: I've studied several different peoples around the world; only two of them were black. I married a white woman. It's absurd! I— Jesus! *(He moves around the room, flustered.)*

MICHAELA: I should have figured it out as soon as I walked into your office the first time.

ALAN: Figured out what?

MICHAELA: Your fascination with Africans. And your appropriation of their—

ALAN: Appropriation?!

MICHAELA: You think those masks were meant to hang on office walls?

ALAN: *(Refers to the Sri Lankan mask.)* You've got one right there!

MICHAELA: That was a *gift*; not part of a collection.

(ALAN throws his hands up, frustrated, and walks away.)

(MICHAELA continues, sharply, with feeling.)

MICHAELA: What do you remember about our affair, Alan?

ALAN: I…I remember the arguments and the sex…

MICHAELA: You remember the sex, of course. Under the watchful gaze of your African fertility figure.

ALAN: So…?

MICHAELA: I remember one particular night, during an unusually *un*heated conversation that *preceded* our lovemaking. We were talking about our research goals.

ALAN: *(Doesn't remember)* Alright…

MICHAELA: I was telling you about my interest in sub-Saharan women.

ALAN: I don't remember...

MICHAELA: How I wanted to go to Mali or The Gambia to study initiation rites among the Bondo secret societies. You don't remember that? That I wanted to study the very women, the exact population you ended up making the subject of your research.

ALAN: *(Careful)* So what? You're saying...?

MICHAELA: You used me, Alan.

ALAN: Hold on—

MICHAELA: You used me and you—

ALAN: You think I was going out with you so I could steal your ideas?

MICHAELA: We did not go out! We stayed in!

ALAN: Okay!

MICHAELA: I think you came after me because you were aroused by the thought of sex with a black woman—

ALAN: Wh—?!

MICHAELA: —and when I told you about my interest in Bondo, I unwittingly opened a whole new world of exploration.

ALAN: *(Openly flustered)* Oh my god...!

MICHAELA: You deny it?

ALAN: Of course I deny--! It's— You're misinterpreting why I—

MICHAELA: Am I?

ALAN: Yes! That's not—

MICHAELA: I shared that research goal with you in confidence. You were so encouraging at the time.

ALAN: Exactly!

MICHAELA: It never occurred to me you would claim it as your own.

ALAN: *You broke things off, Michaela!* So a couple of years later I— You could have done the research. Nobody stopped you. *I* certainly didn't.

MICHAELA: You betrayed my trust, Alan!

ALAN: *(Realizes)* Is that what this is?

MICHAELA: Hmm?

ALAN: You brought me in here to chastise me for—?

MICHAELA: *(Opens her arms wide, slightly mocking)* Bravo, Alan!

ALAN: You *chose not* to go to Africa and study Bondo initiation rites, Michaela. So the fact that I *did* is really irrelevant.

(Beat)

MICHAELA: What I'm saying, Alan, is I think you have a bit of a blind spot where your interests are concerned.

(Pause)

ALAN: I did not. Steal. Your ideas. *(Takes a deep breath)* But… *(Vaguely confessional)* Was there a little added intrigue for me, about sleeping with a black woman? Sure! When I met you, I'd been with a total of maybe five women, including my wife, and all of them were white. Growing up as an intellectual kid in the middle of Jewish suburbia, *all* girls were exotic to me! And yes, you were a little more so.

MICHAELA: There. That wasn't so hard, now was it?

ALAN: And, for the record, I'm pretty sure I was just as exotic to you.

MICHAELA: Perhaps… *(She allows the hint of a smile to break through, as she shakes her head.)*

ALAN: I'm surprised we continued to see each other as long as we did.

MICHAELA: So am I.

ALAN: Was there anything about our…relationship—

MICHAELA: Call it what it was, Alan! An affair.

ALAN: Alright! Is there anything about— *Me* that you liked?

MICHAELA: I liked the way your mind worked. I liked your intensity. I liked how much interest you showed in me.

ALAN: Even though I was, apparently, fetishizing you.

MICHAELA: Well. I didn't know that at the time.

(ALAN *takes a deep breath.*)

MICHAELA: I think I might have fallen in love.

ALAN: You think you might actually *have*, or you think you *would* have…?

(MICHAELA *gives away nothing.* ALAN, *unsettled, moves to the window and looks out for a long moment. Quietly, without turning around and with an almost boyish innocence.*)

ALAN: Do you really think I fetishize black women?

MICHAELA: I think there's a pattern worth exploring, Alan.

(*Pause*)

ALAN: (*Still looking out the window*) You said earlier it's not an accident that we chose different paths.

(*No response from* MICHAELA)

ALAN: The thing is… We both wanted to study *people*. Because we both know that even with our ability to explain so many mysteries of the universe, *people* remain the most…impenetrable piece of the puzzle.

We can map the human genome and still have no idea why we do half the things we do…

MICHAELA: Very true.

ALAN: I certainly don't know why I do half the things I do.

(MICHAELA *smiles.*)

ALAN: Despite our intelligence, or maybe because of it, the fact is…we're hopelessly irrational.

MICHAELA: *(With a soft smile)* Definitely one of *your* kind of facts.

(ALAN *hears this, but doesn't respond.* MICHAELA *watches him for a long moment.*)

MICHAELA: I have a proposal, Alan.

ALAN: A proposal?

MICHAELA: With regard to your paper.

ALAN: *(Still looking out the window, with sarcastic lack of enthusiasm)* Great.

MICHAELA: I would like you to delay publication, while I commission a second, independent study of the women who practice female genital mutilation—

(ALAN *turns halfway back, eyes closed with irritation, but stops himself from speaking.*)

MICHAELA: I'd like to send a doctoral candidate in anthropology -- a woman from Sierra Leone – I'd like to send her to all the countries where you conducted your research.

ALAN: You've already talked to people about this?

MICHAELA: Her study could accompany yours; it would either dispute, or, I suppose, verify your findings.

ALAN: When you say commission…?

MICHAELA: I've got some discretionary funds. And friends high up at 28 Too Many and the New Field Foundation who would happily support this venture.

ALAN: I'm sure you could rally a whole army of supporters.

MICHAELA: So, what do you say?

ALAN: It would be a colossal waste of resources.

MICHAELA: But if this bright young woman were to draw entirely different conclusions from yours, the study would prove extremely worthwhile.

ALAN: To *you*.

MICHAELA: To the world!

ALAN: Jesus! Michaela! You think some twenty-five year-old, with probably no field experience and no credentials—

MICHAELA: She's twenty-eight, and she'll have guidance from her advisor—

ALAN: —you think she's going to execute a credible study just because she's an African woman?

MICHAELA: I believe she'll gain the trust of her subjects.

ALAN: *(Laughs)* Some of the ethnic populations there are more hostile toward each other than they are toward outsiders. Even pasty white folks like me! This is outrageous!

MICHAELA: Why?

ALAN: For all I know, you'll just have some "graduate student" concoct a fake study to debunk mine!

MICHAELA: Now why would I do that?

ALAN: You know that another study is personally motivated.

MICHAELA: Personally—?

ALAN: You just accused me of stealing your research idea!

(MICHAELA *turns away.*)

ALAN: Why not just let things play out? My paper will go through the peer review process. If my findings provoke some detractors to do *legitimate* research of their own, great! We'll have a broader conversation. But this! *This* is—

MICHAELA: What?

ALAN: This is the petty stuff you said you're trying to avoid. There isn't an established scholar at this university who wouldn't have the same reaction.

MICHAELA: Would it help to meet her?

ALAN: Meet who?

MICHAELA: The doctoral candidate.

ALAN: It doesn't matter who it is, Michaela. My objection isn't to this student you're proposing.

MICHAELA: Good. (*She moves toward the door.*) Then I'm going to invite her in.

ALAN: What?

MICHAELA: She's in the other room. The woman I've been telling you about.

ALAN: She's here?! (*Realizes:*) Wait! That was her, sitting outside your office?!

MICHAELA: I assume so, yes.

ALAN: So this is what? Some kind of ambush?

MICHAELA: Not at all. (*She is poised to open the door.*)

ALAN: You had this whole thing planned out, didn't you?

MICHAELA: I actually haven't spoken with her yet.

ALAN: Right!

MICHAELA: She doesn't even know why I've asked her to come. She doesn't know about your research. She doesn't know about the protest.

ALAN: Why should I believe you? You haven't been straight about anything else today.

(But MICHAELA *has opened the door. She talks to someone in the next room:)*

MICHAELA: Lydia?

LYDIA: *(Faintly heard off-stage)* Yes.

ALAN: *(Under his breath)* This is unbelievable!

MICHAELA: Would you mind coming in?

LYDIA: Okay.

*(*MICHAELA *holds the door open, as* LYDIA NAMANDU *enters.)*

MICHAELA: *(Extends her hand to* LYDIA*)* I'm Michaela Richards, Dean of Arts & Sciences.

LYDIA: *(Shakes* MICHAELA*'s hand)* Hello.

MICHAELA: And this is Dr Alan Friedman, professor of psychology.

LYDIA: Really? *(Extends her hand to* ALAN.*)* I am a great admirer of your work.

ALAN: *(Shakes* LYDIA*'s hand)* Ah. Well, thanks. It's nice to meet you.

LYDIA: It is an honor, really.

ALAN: *(Refers to his nose)* I like your nose ring.

*(*MICHAELA *shoots* ALAN *a look.)*

LYDIA: It's actually a stud.

ALAN: Ah, right. Sorry.

MICHAELA: So: Lydia…Namandu?

LYDIA: *(Correcting the emphasis)* Namandu.

MICHAELA: And you're from Sierra Leone, is that right?

LYDIA: Yes.

MICHAELA: You're working with Dr Salters?

LYDIA: He is my thesis advisor.

ALAN: I know Leo. What's the topic of your thesis?

LYDIA: *(Cautious)* I…mmm…why do you want to know?

ALAN: Just thought I'd ask.

LYDIA: I…haven't settled on a specific topic yet. I've been a little indecisive…

ALAN: *(Smiles, knowingly)* Like every other grad student.

LYDIA: I guess I haven't found my voice yet.

ALAN: Your voice?

LYDIA: Dr Salters says that being a scholar is like being an artist; you need to find your own voice.

MICHAELA: That sounds like something Leo would say.

LYDIA: Like you, Dr Friedman. Everyone knows what your work is about.

ALAN: *(Smiles, knowingly)* Well…

LYDIA: You deliberately take the unconventional, unpopular point of view.

ALAN: That's not exactly—

MICHAELA: He certainly does.

LYDIA: I think my thesis will be something having to do with the elderly in America.

ALAN: *(Surprised)* Okay.

LYDIA: I'm interested in how the nuclear American family has evolved further away from multi-generational and communal living.

(ALAN *and* MICHAELA *share a look.*)

LYDIA: And how this American practice of separating the elders from their families and putting them in old age homes has become a cultural norm.

MICHAELA: Dr Friedman was just telling me about how he set his parents up in an assisted living facility.

LYDIA: Ah. Maybe I could interview you.

ALAN: *(Feeling slightly accused)* Uh, sure, but…I, um…I wouldn't call it a *practice*…

LYDIA: But it is extremely common here, yes?

ALAN: I suppose…

LYDIA: We do not understand this. In Sierra Leone, the grandparents, even the *great* grandparents, are an important part of the family. *And* the home. It seems so cruel and unnecessary to send them away when they need you the most. *(Realizes she may have said too much.)* So… That is the starting point of my research.

ALAN: *(Deflects)* Well. That's not why you're here. *(To* MICHAELA*)* Right? You asked Lydia here to—

MICHAELA: *(Stares daggers at* ALAN.*)* Alan…

ALAN: What? I was just moving things along.

MICHAELA: *I* invited Lydia here. I would appreciate it if you'd let me tell her why.

ALAN: *(With a sarcastic flourish)* You're the Dean!

LYDIA: *(Confused and uncomfortable)* I think, maybe, I should go…

MICHAELA: *(To* LYDIA*)* Don't mind him, Lydia.

ALAN: *(With a joking smile) She* never does, so—

MICHAELA: Alan.

ALAN: Sorry!

MICHAELA: Let's try to behave like adults, shall we?

(ALAN *bristles.*)

MICHAELA: Now, Lydia: You come highly recommended from Leo and some of my other colleagues in the department.

LYDIA: Really?

MICHAELA: *(Nods, with a smile)* I've invited you here today to consider a research opportunity. It's a little unusual, I know, but please hear me out.

LYDIA: Okay.

MICHAELA: Dr Friedman has written a paper, unpublished for the moment, based on research he conducted in...several—

ALAN: Four.

MICHAELA: —countries in Africa.

ALAN: The Gambia, Mali, Sierra Leone, and the Sudan.

LYDIA: Okay...

ALAN: What part of Sierra Leone are you from?

LYDIA: My family is in Madina, outside of Freetown.

ALAN: *(Smiles)* I know Madina.

MICHAELA: His research team interviewed hundreds of women and girls in those countries about their feelings and attitudes toward the practice of female... circumcision.

LYDIA: *(Suddenly stiffens, looks at* ALAN*) You* did this research?

ALAN: I led the study. I didn't do the actual interviews.

MICHAELA: And their findings were surprising, even to them.

(MICHAELA *looks to* ALAN *for approval, and he nods in-kind.)*

MICHAELA: They found that a majority of the women they interviewed—

ALAN: Virtually *all* of the women.

MICHAELA: —had a very positive view of the practice, and believe it to be a physical and spiritual improvement.

(LYDIA *remains tense.*)

MICHAELA: So. I would like to commission you to conduct an independent study with the same population. I've discussed this with Leo, and he's agreed to advise the project.

LYDIA: *(Surprised)* You want me to conduct the same study?

MICHAELA: It would be designed and conducted by you.

LYDIA: That *is* unusual.

ALAN: I'll say!

MICHAELA: *(Holds up her hand signaling* ALAN *to be quiet)* Alan.

LYDIA: And you are assuming that because I am an African woman I might get a different response from the subjects.

MICHAELA: Significantly different, yes.

LYDIA: *(Overly formal)* With all respect, I don't think I should do this study for you.

MICHAELA: Why not?

LYDIA: *(She moves toward the door.)* I am truly honored that you considered me for—

MICHAELA: Lydia—

LYDIA: Thank you for the invitation. I am very pleased to meet you both. *(She exits.)*

(MICHAELA *shoots an angry look at* ALAN.)

ALAN: What did *I* do?

(MICHAELA *exits.* ALAN *closes his eyes and takes a deep breath.*)

MICHAELA: *(From off)* Lydia. Please come back. I want to hear your concerns.

LYDIA: *(From off)* I don't want to get in the middle of something between you and Dr Friedman.

MICHAELA: That's not the—

LYDIA: I didn't know why you invited me.

ALAN: *(To himself)* You're not alone, hon!

MICHAELA: *(From off)* I'm sorry about that. Really. But please hear me out. And after we talk, if you still don't want to pursue this project, I promise I will do nothing but support you.

(A pause. LYDIA *returns to the office, followed by* MICHAELA.*)*

MICHAELA: So. Lydia: Why don't you think you should do this research?

LYDIA: *(Clear and careful)* You know that the women who practice this initiation are part of a secret society.

MICHAELA: Yes, both Dr Friedman and I are familiar with Bondo.

LYDIA: *(Correcting* MICHAELA's *pronunciation) Bondo.* It is secret for a reason.

MICHAELA: I understand.

ALAN: She's saying it's not—

MICHAELA: I know what she's saying.

LYDIA: I don't know how Dr Friedman was able to convince women to talk to him, but for *me*… As a native of Sierra Leone, they would feel that I was betraying them. Stealing their stories and sharing their secrets.

MICHAELA: We're not interested in stories; we're only interested in data.

LYDIA: I understand that, but--

MICHAELA: I expect I can get you enough funding to cover all the basics – travel, housing, visas, fees for assistants and translators, and, of course, *your* fee…

LYDIA: Is it worth so much money for a second study on the same population? Funding like that could pay for a lot of food and medicine, which would be much more valuable to the women.

MICHAELA: I'm not in a position to get funding for food and medicine. My resources are purely academic.

LYDIA: I understand.

MICHAELA: It's a generous offer.

LYDIA: Yes…

ALAN: *(To* LYDIA, *refers to* MICHAELA*)* And you'll get a really nice letter of recommendation from—

MICHAELA: Alan—

ALAN: What? That's the kind of endorsement grad students dream about.

MICHAELA: *(Ignores* ALAN, *turns to* LYDIA*)* Well…?

LYDIA: I am guessing that many African peoples feel the same way; that so much money is being spent on European and American scientists to study our cultures, our religions, our social structures… But what do the studies really do for the people who are studied? Maybe people who read the New York Times or listen to NPR become more aware of some part of our culture. And maybe a few who read about us make a small donation to a cause. But mostly what it does is satisfy a curiosity.

ALAN: That's a little dismissive—

MICHAELA: *(Holds up her hand again)* I hope that the work of science, in general, advances our understanding of the world so that we can improve our conditions. My hope for *this* study, for instance, is that the world might understand, more fully, the lives of so many African women.

LYDIA: There is another student in the department. She's from Turkey, but she's doing work on fertility rituals—

MICHAELA: Lydia. Look: I know this is a sensitive issue, and that many women may be hesitant to participate—

LYDIA: That's not—

MICHAELA: —but I'm guessing that someone on the inside, someone like yourself—

LYDIA: *No, Dean Richards. (A decision)* I think I can save you all that money and time and effort.

MICHAELA: Okay…

LYDIA: Dr Friedman's findings are correct.

MICHAELA: *(Taken aback)* They are?

LYDIA: My understanding is that the practice is quite different in The Sudan. The surgeries are more…

MICHAELA: Severe. They're more severe. Type *III*.

ALAN: Infibulation.

MICHAELA: *(Overlapping, with irritation)* Infibulation, yes. They excise the clitoris and the labia and stitch together the edges of the vulva.

ALAN: *(Careful)* Actually, nobody excises the *entire* clitoris. I mean, you'd die! In some cultures, they excise the externally protruding glans.

LYDIA: Yes. Infibulation is, as you say, much more severe. And that is not what we practice in Sierra Leone. I can't speak with authority for women in The Sudan, but I know that initiation into *Bondo* makes women feel their bodies are more beautiful; more feminine; more civilized; and more honorable.

ALAN: Well, well, well!

MICHAELA: How do you know this?

LYDIA: *(Careful)* It is not something that is talked about, especially to outsiders, but…it is generally known and accepted. Most women of Sierra Leone, they practice the initiation with great joy and purpose. And we take pride in deciding the future of our own bodies.

MICHAELA: *Our* bodies?

LYDIA: Yes, *our* bodies. I am initiated.

MICHAELA: *(Aghast)* What?!

LYDIA: I am initiated. Circumcised.

ALAN: Wow. This is so not the conversation I expected when I came here today. *(To* LYDIA*)* I should really have you come talk to my class.

MICHAELA: Alan!

*(*ALAN *throws up his hands and walks away.)*

LYDIA: *(Expresses a great sense of relief)* This is the first time I have told anyone here in the U S.

MICHAELA: *(Genuinely sympathetic) You* were forced to submit—?

LYDIA: *(Flinches)* No one forced me.

MICHAELA: But you must have been—

LYDIA: *No one forced me.* I am from an educated family. My father is a professor and my mother works in a medical office. I accepted the call to be initiated by choice.

MICHAELA: Were you presented with alternatives? Did you understand the risks?

LYDIA: My mother talked to me when I was very young about Bondo, about what it means to be a woman, and that is what I wanted for myself. I hope to one day have a daughter who will be initiated into Bondo. And it will be her choice as well.

MICHAELA: Well, I *am* a mother. And I could never— *(Suddenly at a loss)* How could you want that for your daughter?!

LYDIA: There is nothing I would want more.

MICHAELA: *(Trying to manage her distress)* We'll see how easy it is for you to say that when you have an actual child, a *girl* whom you love and cherish and whom you are responsible for. *(She retrieves a framed photo from her desk and shows it to* LYDIA.*)* My daughter, Naila, is fifteen years old. And there's nothing I wouldn't do for her. God knows there have been many times when I wanted to *insist* that she follow the same path as me. Or that she specifically *shouldn't* follow the same path. But I held my tongue and let her decide. Every time!

ALAN: And now she wants to be a poet!

LYDIA: *(References the photo)* She is very beautiful, your daughter. She looks like a friend of mine from university.

*(*MICHAELA *stifles a reaction)*

LYDIA: I'm sure you are a wonderful mother.

MICHAELA: Please, don't—

LYDIA: And it is good of you not to insist on anything. I would not insist on anything either. Including initiation. But that is what I would *want* for my daughter. And I imagine that she would want it for herself.

MICHAELA: You believe that cutting your daughter's--
That *allowing* her to be cut is a good thing?

LYDIA: It is not about permission—

MICHAELA: Because if you do, you've been—

LYDIA: What? I've been what?

MICHAELA: I don't know. Coerced? Brainwashed?

LYDIA: *(She stiffens again.)* I'm sorry, Dean Richards.

*(*MICHAELA *pulls back slightly.* LYDIA *hands back the photo.)*

LYDIA: This is all we hear from Western women: We must be brainwashed to allow ourselves to be violated; to be deprived of such pleasure. Such ecstasy. I have had boyfriends and I have had orgasms. I don't know what *more* pleasure I may be missing. How can I? How can *you*? But I do know that no amount of pleasure is more important than my dignity as a woman. I think that is a fundamental difference between our cultures.

MICHAELA: It's not an either/or! Dignity and pleasure are not incompatible! You shouldn't have to choose between them!

LYDIA: You are right. And we do not have to make that choice in Bondo.

MICHAELA: And it's not only the pleasure itself; it's the *freedom* to *experience* it.

LYDIA: Yes, you Americans cherish your freedom, above all.

MICHAELA: You say that as if it's a bad thing.

LYDIA: Not at all. I admire your singular passion for freedom. It is what makes this country so popular! In Sierra Leone, we hold several values in equal importance: Freedom, dignity, community. *(Beat)* You know, when I first came here three years ago, I had hoped to study one of your American practices that might be comparable to Bondo; a cultural tradition or ritual that is sacred, that has deep communal meaning, and that is passed down from one generation to the next; from grandmothers to mothers to daughters. But I could not identify one.

MICHAELA: Well, I'm glad we don't practice *your* tradition!

LYDIA: Of course. But to have none of your own? *(She shakes her head.)*

MICHAELA: Did your mother drag you, kicking and screaming, to the ceremony?

LYDIA: No kicking or screaming. But I was scared. Of course, I was scared.

MICHAELA: She terrorized you!

LYDIA: No. She supported me and…inspired me. With so many other women there to celebrate my initiation. My grandmother, my aunts, my teachers, my older sister.

MICHAELA: That's—!

LYDIA: It's what?

MICHAELA: I'm sorry, Lydia, but that is…grotesque.

LYDIA: I see children here, crying, when they are being dragged to the dentist. Are they being terrorized?

(MICHAELA looks sharply at LYDIA.)

LYDIA: It is healthy to visit the dentist, I understand. But mostly, it is to make our teeth look nice and shiny white, yes? So many children crying and screaming at least once every year, just for nice looking teeth!

MICHAELA: It's more than— *(She stops herself. Closes her eyes)* Having your teeth cleaned is not the same as having your clitoris cut off.

ALAN: Actually, more and more women in Australia and the U K—women of a certain class and wealth, of course—are paying for "designer vaginas." You know, cosmetic surgeries that end up looking pretty much like those of circumcised women.

(LYDIA *and* MICHAELA *stare at* ALAN.)

ALAN: What? I'm— *(He realizes the futility of his protest.)* I'll just shut up.

MICHAELA: What about your father, Lydia? You're telling me Daddy just sat back and let his little girl get mutilated?

LYDIA: Please…! *(Manages the provocation)* You want to know about my father? One night, a few weeks before the ceremony, when I was feeling unsure, I asked him how he would feel if I was not initiated. He told me that when he was thirteen and physically mature, all he wanted was to be a man. His older cousins were going to be initiated, but the elders thought my father was too young. He threw a fit and demanded they let him be initiated, too, and so they did. I asked my father: "Wasn't it painful?" He laughed. "Painful? It was the most painful thing I have ever experienced in my life. It took a month to fully recover."

ALAN: *(Shivers)* Eeesh!

LYDIA: "But during that time," he said,"the elders taught us so many things—about the history of our people, about what it means to be a man, about how to treat women, how to have sex, how to drink beer, how to own property, how to face up to painful things in life and be fearless. And in that month, we bonded with each other, the other boys and I. I feel closer to those men who were initiated with me than anyone else in the world." He told me he never understood why boys are circumcised as babies in the West. "Why would you do that to an infant?" he said. "The pain will be meaningless to him. He will be too young to learn anything or appreciate the significance of his initiation. There will be no one sharing his experience; no one with whom he can form life-long bonds."

MICHAELA: There are other ways to form bonds that are less painful and don't involve permanent damage to the body.

ALAN: *(To* LYDIA, *referring to* MICHAELA) *This* we agree on.

LYDIA: I think, perhaps, your protest is more about pain than it is about gender.

MICHAELA: It's about the treatment of women.

LYDIA: Did you know that among my people, the Kono, our original creator is female? And that men are detached from her? It is actually your Judeo-Christian religion that is patriarchal, not ours.

MICHAELA: I'm an atheist.

LYDIA: I'm not surprised. But your culture has been formed around the values of Christianity, no? Your male god of Abraham created man first, from whom Eve was derived. In the Torah and the Bible, women are second class citizens; sometimes only property. And there is great emphasis on control over female sexuality: virginity, chastity, fidelity.

(ALAN *and* MICHAELA *share an awkward look.*)

LYDIA: In my country, it is true that women cannot freely choose their husbands, but wives are not required or even expected to be faithful to their husbands. They are free to take young male lovers to satisfy them, sexually, and they remind their husbands that no man *owns* their vaginas. I'm not sure it is possible for you to understand how we think. Both men and women in Sierra Leone are treated equally. Does this surprise you?

MICHAELA: If it's actually true.

LYDIA: We are both circumcised, and for the same reasons. To fully embrace womanhood, we must eliminate the vestige of the protruding male organ. But every boy must also eliminate the vestige of the covered female organ to become a man.

ALAN: So, in Sierra Leone, I'd be welcomed as a full-fledged man, while you—

MICHAELA: *(Holds up her hand)* Please, Alan—

ALAN: —you'd still be considered what?

LYDIA: She would be gboroka.

MICHAELA: I don't give a damn how I'd be thought of in Sierra Leone!

LYDIA: And there is no reason that you should.

MICHAELA: *(With effort to be pleasant)* Look. Lydia: Even if I could accept the cultural differences, which, mind you, I *don't*, I can't abide the medical risks being taken by so many African girls. Isn't it a fact that F G M can cause severe bleeding and problems urinating? And later on, difficulties with child bearing, infections, infertility—

LYDIA: Of course, it *can*, Dean Richards. And I'm sure each of those things happens on occasion. Those are the stories that make it to C N N and N P R. The stories that lead to documentaries. I think those stories are the rare exceptions.

MICHAELA: Even if that is the case, the exceptions are not acceptable.

LYDIA: I agree with you. Really, I do.

MICHAELA: We're talking about delicate surgeries on extremely sensitive organs, conducted with primitive instruments, and performed by women who are not trained physicians.

LYDIA: *(Nods her head)* You've seen the images of hysterical girls, running with blood dripping down their legs.

MICHAELA: Yes.

LYDIA: Older women wielding unsterilized razor blades.

MICHAELA: Yes!

LYDIA: Maybe even shards of glass or jagged stones.

MICHAELA: Yes! Exactly!

LYDIA: These images, they may be truthful. But are they the exception or the rule? I can tell you that the surgeries in my community are an ancient practice conducted by highly trained elders—Soweis—with properly sterilized instruments.

MICHAELA: Maybe the practice in *your* community is the exception, not the rule.

LYDIA: May*be*. But even if this was the case, and initiation rites across Africa were as dangerous as you believe they are, shouldn't you want to make them safer?

MICHAELA: No! That would only encourage the practice.

LYDIA: Like abortions.

MICHAELA: What?

LYDIA: Before Roe versus Wade, when abortions in this country were done illegally in bathrooms and basements, with knives and coat hangers, did you want the practice to stop or did you want the practice to become safer?

ALAN: *(Inappropriately triumphant)* This is *my* point exactly!

MICHAELA: *(Holds up her hand)* Alan.

ALAN: If you're pro-choice, Michaela—

MICHAELA: *(Holds up her hand)* Alan!

ALAN: —someone who champions a woman's right to determine what to do with her own body, put your money where your mouth is: *(Refers to* LYDIA*)* Let them choose!

MICHAELA: *(Holds up her hand)* Alan, please!

ALAN: Enough with the hand!

(A charged moment between ALAN *and* MICHAELA. *He looks at* LYDIA, *realizes what she sees, and tries to manage the heat of his frustration.)*

ALAN: Excuse me a moment.

*(*ALAN *exits.* LYDIA *and* MICHAELA *look at each other for a moment. He reappears, a bit sheepish.)*

ALAN: Where *is* the bathroom?

MICHAELA: Down the hall, on the left.

*(*MICHAELA *turns to* LYDIA, *newly poised.)*

MICHAELA: I'm sorry you had to see that. This research of Dr Friedman's has struck a nerve.

LYDIA: I understand.

MICHAELA: I'm not sure that you do.

LYDIA: You have a history.

MICHAELA: Yes. But that's not the issue.

LYDIA: You are upset by his findings.

MICHAELA: I don't believe his findings.

LYDIA: You do not believe I should be allowed to make the choice that I have made? You think that I am foolish, misguided, ignorant.

MICHAELA: What I think, Lydia, is that you didn't make that choice as freely as you think you did.

LYDIA: How would you know?

MICHAELA: I know that women often think they are *choosing* to stay in an abusive relationship. That they are *choosing* to stay in a job where their boss harasses them. *Choosing* to look sexy for *themselves* when they put on heels and show their cleavage and cover their faces in makeup. I have no doubt that women make *conscious* choices, all the time, to do things that I might see as harmful or foolish. The question is whether they know, *really know*, that the alternatives are viable. If you don't believe you'll be truly accepted or truly safe or truly free by making a different choice, are you *truly choosing*?

(LYDIA *quietly takes the hit, as* MICHAELA *feels somewhat emboldened.*)

LYDIA: *(A decision to go on the offensive for the first time.)* May I ask you something, Dean Richards? I assume you are uncircumcised?

MICHAELA: Of course I am!

LYDIA: You can't imagine, can you, that I am as revolted by your choice as you are by mine?

MICHAELA: This is not about—

LYDIA: Can you tell me: Why do you want such unsightly, misshapen genitals?

MICHAELA: *(Shocked)* Excuse me?!

LYDIA: All they are, really, is an unwelcome reminder of the male organ.

(MICHAELA *is speechless.*)

LYDIA: I want a full female identity. I want to feel connected to a social network of powerful adult women, past and present.

MICHAELA: You don't need to have surgery to feel that connection.

LYDIA: *You* don't. But *I do.*

MICHAELA: Just because you were taught this by your family, by your elders—

LYDIA: *You* were taught things by *yours.*

MICHAELA: —doesn't make it right.

LYDIA: I didn't know any differently until my final year at secondary school. A girl from the U K—Clarissa Meachum—she brought an adult magazine to school, and the other girls and I crowded into a corner of the locker room after physical education class. Page after page of beautiful white women with such skinny bodies, completely naked, and all I could think was "what kind of civilized mothers allow their daughters to keep themselves like that down there?!" *(She looks directly at* MICHAELA.*)* To be honest, Dean Richards, just knowing that you are an uncircumcised woman, that fact alone, makes you seem...undignified.

MICHAELA: *(Tries to manage her feelings) You* think *I* am undignified?!

LYDIA: How does it feel to be judged for something that is so acceptable in your culture?

*(*MICHAELA *is stunned. She moves away and gathers herself.)*

*(*ALAN *returns, disrupting the silence.)*

ALAN: Lydia: I was just thinking... *(Laughs to himself)* While I was in the bathroom, right? Do you know how we were able to get African women to talk to us? We had developed a list of about thirty questions. You know, things like "how did you feel about yourself – your body, your spirit -- before and after circumcision? What kinds of pressures did you feel and from whom?" But we learned, very quickly, that most women were not comfortable offering details or descriptions of anything, just as you suggested. So instead, we created a long list of questions that could simply be answered "yes" or "no". "Did you feel pressure from anyone before the ritual? Did you make the decision on your own? Did you feel differently about yourself after circumcision? Was it a positive feeling?" That's really all we needed, and they seemed to feel like they were giving less away.

LYDIA: *(Not a compliment)* That was a clever strategy.

ALAN: *(Making this an overtly teachable moment)* Well, a big part of our job is figuring out what other peoples' triggers are, their fears, their boundaries.

LYDIA: You are an expert on that.

ALAN: *(Badly feigning humility)* Well…

LYDIA: But you are also a poacher, Dr Friedman.

ALAN: A poacher?!

LYDIA: You think that because you are acting in the name of 'science' it makes you more honorable? That because you found a way for women to answer 'yes' and 'no' makes you any less of a thief?

ALAN: I—

LYDIA: That profiting off of stolen secrets, instead of elephant tusks, is any less harmful?

(ALAN doesn't know what to say.)

MICHAELA: *(Turns to LYDIA, with a new tack)* Lydia: You said that you haven't told anyone else here about your…status.

LYDIA: No…

MICHAELA: Not your roommate? Not your…partner?

LYDIA: I…

MICHAELA: Well?

LYDIA: I-- I don't see why that is important.

MICHAELA: I just imagine it's not something one can hide forever.

LYDIA: *(Quietly.)* I don't have a roommate.

MICHAELA: Do you have a partner?

ALAN: Michaela—

MICHAELA: What? It's not a complicated question. Does she have a partner?

ALAN: It's kind of a *personal* question. *(To* LYDIA*)* You don't have to talk about—

MICHAELA: This is not an interrogation. I'm just curious. Are you seeing someone?

ALAN: *(To* MICHAELA*, referring to* LYDIA*)* And I'm just telling her she doesn't have to—

LYDIA: Thank you, Dr Friedman, but I can decide for myself. *(Beat. To* MICHAELA*)* Yes. I'm seeing someone.

MICHAELA: Is he or she American?

LYDIA: *(Quietly)* He is.

MICHAELA: What does he think about how you keep yourself "down there?"

ALAN: *(Alarmed)* Michae—

MICHAELA: *(Signals him to keep quiet)* He must have had some kind of reaction.

LYDIA: No…

MICHAELA: No?!

LYDIA: Not yet…

MICHAELA: *(With sarcasm)* So, you're just a typical graduate student practicing abstinence?!

*(*LYDIA*, head down, says nothing.)*

MICHAELA: Ha! He doesn't have a clue what he's getting into, does he?!

ALAN: This is highly inappropriate, Michaela. You could lose your job—

MICHAELA: *(Sharply, to ALAN)* She's a grown woman, Alan. She doesn't need your protection.

LYDIA: I don't think he'll have a problem...

MICHAELA: No? So why have you kept him from seeing your *initiated parts*? If you don't think he'll have a problem with it. *Why*, Lydia? Because you know your boyfriend will be shocked. Outraged. *Revolted* by your *mutilated*—

LYDIA: *(With surprising ferocity)* Do not tell me I am mutilated! I am NOT mutilated!!

(A charged silence)

LYDIA: My boyfriend. This one...is different...

MICHAELA: Different from whom?

LYDIA: It doesn't matter...

MICHAELA: No, please! Tell me.

LYDIA: Different from...others in the past.

MICHAELA: Ah. There were other American boys who weren't quite so open-minded.

(LYDIA says nothing.)

MICHAELA: Why do you think African mothers are having their girls initiated younger and younger, Lydia? Why is the practice steadily declining?

ALAN: In very small numbers, maybe...

MICHAELA: There's a trend, Alan. You know this: Fewer and fewer women every year.

LYDIA: Because African women feel shamed by Western activists.

MICHAELA: Shamed or enlightened?

(LYDIA is quiet.)

MICHAELA: You know that the anti-F G M movement was started by an Egyptian woman, Nawal El Saadawi, and that more and more activists are from *within* these communities.

(LYDIA closes her eyes, clearly managing something painful.)

LYDIA: *(Looks at MICHAELA)* That is how I lost my best friend. Kamali. We were born twelve days apart, and grew up together in Madina. Our families were very close. Kamali and I had planned to be initiated on the same day. We had planned this for many years. *(With obvious disdain)* And then this woman, this *French* woman who worked with an international human rights organization, she got inside Kamali's house and talked to the whole family. And when she left, Kamali had changed. You say she was enlightened. I say she was shamed. She and her family, they judge me the way you do. *(Fighting tears)* And now there is no friendship between us.

(LYDIA looks down, struggling with her feelings. MICHAELA relents. ALAN looks at both of them, then approaches LYDIA.)

ALAN: Lydia: I think it's obvious that Michaela—Dean Richards and I are involved in a kind of debate on all this, and it's also fair to say that it, well, that it has *personal* significance—

MICHAELA: Alan!

ALAN: I don't think what's really troubling her is the practice itself, Lydia. Before she read my paper, she wasn't bothered enough, apparently, to lift a finger—

MICHAELA: I am deeply bothered by it!

ALAN: But you didn't do anything about it.

MICHAELA: I *did* do--!

ALAN: You didn't voice your outrage. You didn't make it a *priority*. You may have wanted to *study* it, like *I* did, but you didn't even do *that*.

LYDIA: I think, Dean Richards, if you had actually gone to Africa and—

MICHAELA: I *did* go to Africa!

LYDIA: I mean, to one of the countries that—

MICHAELA: I went to Africa in [2007] *(Twelve years prior to current year)* to *get my daughter*. I adopted a baby girl from Mali.

LYDIA: So you could spare her the *indignity* of—?

MICHAELA: The *brutality*—

LYDIA: —of F G M?

MICHAELA: Yes.

(Beat)

LYDIA: It has become quite popular: adopting babies from Africa. It used to be only clothing and jewelry, carved ivory and tribal masks that Westerners were interested in. Now it is our children, too.

*(*MICHAELA*, unsettled, moves to the chair behind her desk and sits. Silence)*

ALAN: Think about it, Michaela: A mature young woman just mustered the courage to—

MICHAELA: Oh, now she's mature and courageous? *(To* LYDIA*)* You're not the dilettante he expected you to—

ALAN: *(To* LYDIA*)* I never— *(To* MICHAELA*)* Look: An intelligent woman just explained to you why she does what she does, why she thinks what she thinks, and you're acting like she told you you come from a family of murderers!

MICHAELA: Not murderers…

ALAN: What are you…?

MICHAELA: You really don't get it, do you?

ALAN: Obviously not…

(Pause)

MICHAELA: Lydia and the millions of other African women like her—I'm worried that they will continue to make the same choice.

ALAN: And that's the key: That it's a *choice*.

MICHAELA: That's the problem, Alan. I assumed all those girls were being forced to endure some barbaric initiation rite in order to survive a brutal patriarchal culture. It was yet another example of violent oppression and subjugation of women. *(A difficult admission)* And this is not something I'm proud of, but—I suppose I thought…as long as those *girls* are denied education, rendered helpless, kept servile and submissive by African *men*, I could still imagine them embracing something so repugnant, so invasive, so viscerally unpleasant under duress; and that, in some way, it made them seem *virtuous* and *noble*. They were suffering, like so many other women in history, and their time would still come. *(Now deeply pained)* But if they're educated, and *choosing* to do this to *themselves*— *(Turns to* LYDIA*)* Like you! —I can't imagine them as anything but…

ALAN: But what?

(Beat)

LYDIA: You think we're savages.

(Silence)

(MICHAELA *says nothing.*)

(LYDIA *smiles to herself.*)

LYDIA: You Westerners love being the arbiters of what is considered "civilized". Living inter-generationally is what poor, brown people do. *(Looks at* ALAN*)* Putting your parents in old age homes is what comfortable white people do. Fucking your neighbor's wife in her *straw hut* every now and then is uncivilized, but having an ongoing extra-marital affair at a three-star hotel is practically the American dream.

*(*ALAN *and* MICHAELA *share another look.)*

LYDIA: Surgically removing the foreskin of a man's penis is an act of *great* civility; doing the equivalent to a woman is an act of savagery. You call the operation I underwent in Sierra Leone "mutilation," and it is banned in many countries, but here, where you live, in the center of Western Civilization, it would be my legal prerogative to have the same operation, called "cosmetic surgery," and it would not be *anyone else's business!*

MICHAELA: Being civilized has to do with harnessing our baser, more primal urges so that we can live with each other in greater peace and order.

ALAN: Which is why most cultures began performing circumcision in the first place!

LYDIA: *(To* MICHAELA*)* Yet somehow, when Africans do it, it doesn't feel quite so civilized to you, does it? You have abandoned your African roots, Dean Richards, and embraced the full palette of white, European values, which I'm sure you have proudly passed on to your African daughter. *(She now seems poised, not defensive; newly purposeful.)* I understand why you think we're savages. We have allowed Western activists to tell our story, while we stay silent. *(To herself, with humility)* While I have stayed silent. *(Looks up at* MICHAELA*)* And you think this silence is because we feel ashamed; because we feel humiliated; because we feel afraid to speak out against authorities. Against *men*. But that is not the reason. We are silent because we do not talk about Bondo to outsiders. It is a *secret, sacred sisterhood*.

*(*MICHAELA*'s phone rings.)*

MICHAELA: I apologize. I— *(She picks up the phone and turns to the window as she talks, clearly struggling.)* Hi, sweetie. I'm— Yes, I'm still in the meeting. I'll— No, I'm fine. I'm— *(She takes a deep, pained breath.)* We'll talk later. I'll let you know when I'm leaving. Okay…I love you. *(She ends the call, but continues facing out the window.)*

ALAN: I think we have an opportunity to change the narrative, Lydia. There's too much misinformation out there, and it's time the world knows the facts.

LYDIA: I agree.

ALAN: Once my paper gets published, and the book after that, we can mobilize some media attention and—

LYDIA: No.

ALAN: No, what?

LYDIA: Your paper should stay unpublished.

ALAN: Uhm…I know you haven't read it, but trust me: We're on the same side.

LYDIA: This is not about sides.

ALAN: Right. *(Rephrases)* I think my research represents comprehensive and irrefutable evidence—

LYDIA: I'm sorry, Dr Friedman, but the world should not learn about our beliefs through another anthropological study by another Western scholar. The world beyond academia should hear our story first, and they should hear it from our mouths. Or else we will continue to be just a curiosity. I hope you understand.

ALAN: I'm not suggesting that I put my paper out there first—

LYDIA: It doesn't matter—

ALAN: —but my research could help strengthen *your* efforts to, to inform the public, to— To educate—

LYDIA: The point is, we don't need a study to prove to the world how we feel about our bodies. We can simply say it. Out loud. In public. With conviction and pride. The voices of millions of African women. *(Beat)* I will thank you, Dr Friedman, for keeping your paper to yourself. At least for now. *(She turns to* MICHAELA*)* And I thank *you* for inviting me here, Dean Richards. I am truly grateful for this opportunity.

*(*MICHAELA *says nothing.)*

*(*LYDIA *starts toward the door.)*

ALAN: *(Something suddenly occurs to him.)* Lydia:

*(*LYDIA *stops and turns.* ALAN *makes an effort to be contrite.)*

ALAN: I—I see why it's so important to you that your stories not be told by, well, people like me.

LYDIA: I'm glad.

ALAN: But…

LYDIA: Yes?

ALAN: *You're* planning to study *us.*

(Beat)

LYDIA: *(Without a trace of attitude)* It is our turn, don't you think? *(She exits.)*

*(*MICHAELA *doesn't look at* ALAN, *but continues to stare out the window. He has an impulse to engage her, but doesn't know how to manage it. Independently, at their own pace and in their own way, they both end up looking at the Sri Lankan mask, which somehow seems as if it has been*

watching everything that has transpired. They look at each other, become self-conscious. The mask glows.)

(Lights fade.)

END OF PLAY

CPSIA information can be obtained
at www.ICGtesting.com
Printed in the USA
LVHW081224050921
697025LV00012B/1246

9 780881 458299